You Can Change the World

Richie Hrivnak

YOU
Can change the World!
By Richie Hrivnak

Dedication

This book is dedicated to all the people who inspired me to help those in need and try to change the world. My Mom always believes I can do anything I set my mind to do. My Dad serves our community and has had a positive impact. My Aunt Rori and Uncle Mike have inspired me to be a good example. My Baba is always kind to me and others. She showed me that baking and cooking for others in need can put a smile on their face and show you care. My cousins, Hannah and Leah, are my #1 fans and are always supportive of me. Hannah is going to be a doctor and help others. My Grandma doesn't have a lot of money but is one of the most generous people I know. My Aunt Kris, Uncle Tommy, Katie, Megan and Callie always make me smile and support me in all I do. They all love animals and care for them. My Uncle Dr. Ray is inspiring, because he is successful due to his passion for his work. My Pappys that are in heaven are always in my heart and are helping me to be a better person. My entire family and friends have always been supportive of me and have provided me inspiration for this book! Thank you all!

YOU
Are Bright!

YOU
Are Smart!

YOU
Are Kind!

YOU
Can change the World!

What can
YOU
Do to change the world?

YOU
Can Feed the Hungry by donating food!

YOU
Can Honor Our Veterans by Thanking
them for their Service!

YOU
Can give comfort to a sick or sad child
by giving them a stuffed animal!

You can help the homeless by giving them a blanket so that they aren't cold in the winter!

YOU
Can stand up for someone who is being bullied!

You can help the elderly by
spending time with them!

You can show your neighbor you
care by baking them cookies.

You can rescue an animal by adopting one from a shelter rather than buying one from a store.

You can protect the environment by picking up litter and recycling.

You can help anyone in need by saying a prayer.

There are countless more ways you can help!

What ideas do you have to help change the world?

Who
Can change the world?

YOU
Can change the world!

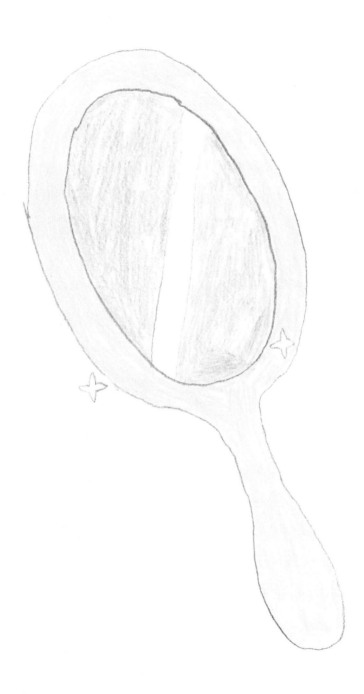

It doesn't matter where you're from!

It doesn't matter what ethnicity you are!

It doesn't matter if you are rich or poor!

Everyone
Can make a positive difference!

Do it Now!
The sooner you start, the bigger

YOU can make!

Copyright © 2017 by Richie Hrivnak. 752294
Library of Congress Control Number: 2017902985

ISBN: Softcover   978-1-5245-8720-8
       Hardcover   978-1-5245-8721-5
       EBook   978-1-5245-8719-2

Print information available on the last page

Rev. date: 02/27/2017

To order additional copies of this book, contact:
Xlibris
1-888-795-4274
www.Xlibris.com
Orders@Xlibris.com

Printed in the United States
By Bookmasters